Pardon Me, But Your References Are Showing!

32 Proven and Fun Activities to Build Reference Skills for Grades 4–8

Second Edition

Teddy Meister

Alleyside
Press

Fort Atkinson, Wisconsin

Published by Alleyside Press, an imprint of Highsmith Press LLC
Highsmith Press
W5527 Highway 106
P.O. Box 800
Fort Atkinson, Wisconsin 53538-0800
1-800-558-2110

© Alleyside Press , 1996
Cover design: Frank Neu

The paper used in this publication meets the minimum requirements of
American National Standard for Information Science — Permanence of
Paper for Printed Library Material. ANSI/NISO Z39.48-1992.

Library of Congress Cataloging-in-Publication Data
    Meister, Teddy.
        Pardon me, but your references are showing! : 32 proven and fun
  activities to build reference skills for grades 4–8 / Teddy Meister. –2nd. ed.
        p. cm.
      Includes bibliographical references and index.
      ISBN 0-917846-80-X (pbk. : alk. paper)
      1. Reference books–Study and teaching (Elementary) I. Title.
  Z1035.1.M45 1996
  028.7' 07–dc20   96-4320
                                         CIP

Contents

"Knowledge is knowing—or knowing where to find out."

Alvin Toffler

"None is poor save him that lacks knowledge."

The Talmud

"An investment in knowledge always pays the best interest."

Benjamin Franklin

"And still I am learning."

Michelangelo Buonarotti

"All we know is still infinitely less than all that still remains unknown."

William Harvey

Introduction

Are you frustrated teaching research skills and introducing students to a variety of reference resources?

Then fascinate students by using the fast, fruitful, fun method of *Pardon Me, But Your References are Showing!*

We live in an information-based society, and knowledge is being collected and organized in vast amounts, ready at our fingertips for instant retrieval. In seconds, we can now find what once might have taken hours or days if we know how and where to search!

In this book students will be involved in searching through a wide variety of library references and using the computer as an information retrieval system. Research will be more meaningful as they will have a real need to search and "*find.*"

Students have fertile imaginations and if they are challenged with interesting assignments, your students will go far to flabbergast and rid you forever of the fatiguing task of teaching the use of reference sources. Teach the concept, then turn them loose by organizing:

- Independent work
- Small groups of cooperative learning
- Total class studies
- Enrichment homework
- An area for whole language
- An application of thinking skills

This book's activities can be mounted and laminated for center use, or set up in individual student "Reference Folders" for the year. Use it as a way to enhance the ongoing instructional program or a method of delivering hands-on skills to gifted and talented students.

How to Use This Book

Before beginning the activities in *Pardon Me, But Your References Are Showing*, check on the availability of needed resources. While many of the exercises can be completed using general encyclopedias, dictionaries, and almanacs commonly found in every library or school media center, users will want to make these activities more interesting by introducing students to a rich variety of reference resources. Users will also want to determine whether additional copies of these materials are available in other libraries to satisfy student needs.

A complete list of the recommended resources in title order is located at the end of this book. Many of these works are frequently revised, so specific editions and copyright dates are omitted. The activities in *Pardon Me, But Your References Are Showing* are general enough to be used with any relatively recent edition. If the user's library or school media center does not have a specific title, several alternative titles are suggested.

Users should encourage their students to use other libraries and school media centers in the local area to complete these activities. This will further enrich their experience, and allow them to become familiar with resources that are not available in their own library or school media center. Users need to determine which libraries are available to their students, and develop a list with the hours of service and addresses for distribution to the students.

If a number of different libraries are available to the students, consider dividing the list, and assign students to visit these libraries to check the availability of titles on the list of recommended resources at the end of this book. Some libraries now have computerized their catalog, and students may be able to search their holdings by dial-up access or by using the Internet and the World Wide Web. Keep this information in a notebook the students can consult when they receive subsequent assignments in this book. If a computer is available, the holdings information might be collected in a simple database.

Another alternative would be to photocopy the list and to forward it to these other libraries. Enclose a brief letter asking whether they would simply place a check mark beside those titles which are available in their collection, and return the list to you. If they don't have a specific title, and time permits, ask whether they might be willing to suggest a similar alternative title that is in their collection. For example, one of the activities suggests the use of the *New Dictionary of American Slang*. Since there are a number of different slang dictionaries, a librarian might suggest a substitute available in that collection. Even if the library does not currently have the time for this research, the librarians will appreciate the advance information about the assignment, and they may be able to assemble the information as time permits.

Some of the activities in this book suggest the use of a computer, and the availability of this equipment and student access to online reference resources should be determined in advance, and added to the notebook or the database of information on other local libraries. If access to computerized resources is limited or nonexistent, alternative print resources are listed with the activities.

While this advance preparation will require time, it is an investment that will be repaid by better results. Some of this can be assigned to the students, who will gain a greater understanding of library research through the process.

Pardon Me, But Your References Are Showing should add a new spark and purpose for students who want to learn, and who need to know how and where to locate specific information. Each of the activities in this book introduces reference resources on a different subject, and each activity contains the following major elements:

Feature

The theme or subject of the activity is briefly noted.

Find

Several reference resources are listed. All of the titles are not required to complete the activity, and alternative resources can be used. However, when substitutions are made, the resources should be consulted to verify that they do relate to the activity, and that they are current.

Fanfare

This brief introduction and reference activity will allow students to demonstrate and offer evidence that they understand how to use the reference resource.

Fabricate

This section suggests a project or product the students can individually or collectively develop using higher cognitive processes. It will allow them to creatively use the information or the research skills they learned in the assigned activities.

As products are completed from Fanfare and Fabricate, consider organizing a Reference Fare Fair. Set up student-developed displays in the library or the school library media center. Have the students list the reference resources they used in developing their product. Invite parents, administrators and other classes to the display. Students can be involved in all aspects of the fair. They can create invitations, design the displays, and provide narratives about the research process as guests visit.

Given the dynamic changes which are taking place in computerized reference resources, and the frequency with which reference books are revised and new titles are published, users of this book will need to regularly review the list of recommended resources. As new titles are added to their library or school media center, the Find section of these activities should be revised. Nonetheless, as of this writing, the recommended resources are either standard titles that students should learn to use, or they are representative of a specific type of reference resource that should be introduced to American school students in grades 4–8, and in comparable age groups in other English-speaking nations.

Ancient Actions

Feature

Ancient events and places

Find

Encyclopedia of Ancient Civilizations

Rand McNally Historical Atlas of the World

Times Concise Atlas of World History

Other Sources: Any encyclopedia such as a recent *World Book* or *Merit Student Encyclopedia*

Fanfare

The ancient city of Troy is believed to have been in Asiatic Turkey. It is associated with the Trojan War and the great stories of Homer, *The Iliad* and *The Odyssey*.

1. List some facts about ancient Troy and its people.

2. Explain and describe an unusual feature of the Trojan War when (in mythology) Paris eloped with Helen!

3. Describe the Greek heroes of the period such as Achilles, Nestor, and Odysseus.

Fabricate

Create a shoebox scene showing what life might have been like in ancient Troy. Or construct a clay model of the Trojan Horse.

(Plan your shoebox scene here.)

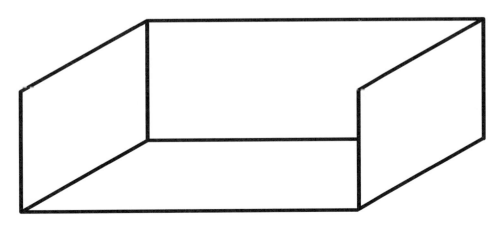

Art and Artists

Feature

Art and Artists.

Find

Art Index.

Encyclopedia of Visual Art

History of Art, by Anthony Janson

A Picture History of Art, by Christopher Lloyd.

Three Hundred Years of American Art, by Michael Zellman.

Other Sources: Any comprehensive art encyclopedia.

Fanfare

Art is the product of that highest capacity of man–the capacity of think and dream. The artist creates that which is in his thoughts and dreams, providing us with a glimpse of life of the period. Great art survives the centuries and barriers of language and custom. All we need to do is look and understand.

Browse and observe the art shown in the books. Select one you could describe to a blind person, using only details appealing to the sense of touch, hearing, taste, or smell. What general mental image can you convey?

Fabricate

Compare the artistic styles of several artists by presenting your opinion of their work. Justify what you say by elaborating on your reasons for liking or not liking their work.

I think that...

Author, Please

Feature

Authors for young people.

Find

Authors of Books for Young People.
Junior Authors and Illustrators.
Junior Book of Authors.
Something About the Author.

Fanfare

Man has been telling stories for thousands of years. Literature is a record of experiences and patterns of life lived as told through the imaginations of authors and poets. Life is interpreted for the reader through the printed word. We enter the author's world, seeing imaginatively through his eyes.

1. Authors frequently choose children as heroes/heroines in works of fiction. Tell about the children created by Charles Dickens, Louisa May Alcott, and Johanna Spyri.

2. Find out about the life of Robert Louis Stevenson and present a short report to the class.

3. Select several stories by contemporary authors. How are they alike? How do they differ?

Fabricate

Collect articles about new books from your local newspaper book section. Mount them into a "literary scrapbook." Which books would adults in your family be interested in reading and why? Collect copies of the "best-seller list" for a special section in the scrapbook.

Career Capers

Feature

Occupational decision-making.

Find

Current Career and Occupational Literature.

Occupational Outlook Handbook.

Other Sources: Any current occupational or career handbook that is comprehensive.

Fanfare

What does a court reporter do? How might someone become an oculist? Think of five possible future career areas that would be interesting as you browse through your chosen source book. Fill in the chart below in order to compare them.

Career	Training Needed	Service Performed

Check the classified ads in the newspaper: How often are openings listed for the career areas you have selected?

Fabricate

Use your imagination and create an unusual career for the year 2050. (It might be servicing the Space Shuttle when it visits Mars!) Write a want ad and design a new tool for use in this career.

Comic Strip Classics

Feature

Comic strips and their origins and history.

Find

Art Index.

The Encyclopedia of Comics, by Hubert Crawford.

Junior Authors and Illustrators.

Other Sources: Any comprehensive history of comic strips.

Fanfare

The combination of exaggerated drawings with a story concerning the same character or set of characters has amused us since 1896! One of the earliest comic strips was "The Yellow Kid." Later, dialogue was added in "balloons" and panels were laid in a line.

Examine works of famous cartoonists and illustrators. Observe how pictures add meaning to stories. Which cartoonists and illustrators appeal to you most? What style of drawing do they use to capture the imagination of readers?

Fabricate

Think of a cartoon character you can create by drawing and experimenting with different facial expressions, hair, and clothing. Will it be an animal or person? Once you are satisfied with your character, develop a story line that can be adapted to comic strip.

Computer Calisthenics

Feature

Computer knowledge.

Find

Windows Tour Guide, by Tom Lichty, or any other computer guide to Windows. MS-DOS on your PC, or any computer guide to MS-DOS.

Fanfare

A computer system is made up of parts called hardware. This includes a monitor, keyboard, mouse, computer processing unit (CPU) and hard drive. Computer software are programs that allow you to do specific applications on the computer, such as games or word processing. Operating systems, such as MS-DOS (Microsoft disk operating system), control the major activities of the computer.

Using a computer with an online service such as Genie, Compuserve and America Online will enable you to become part of a world-wide network of communications. An online service has many resources available. The latest weather and stock market reports, magazines, newspapers, goods for sale, university libraries, hobbies, travel. . . the list is endless. You can even "chat" with other computer users or exchange messages through e-mail. A modem (attached to the computer that converts data into audible tones heard through a telephone) is needed for online services.

Look through the advertisement section of a newspaper for a week and cut out ads from stores selling computers. List them on the chart and do some comparison price shopping. Which one has the features you would like to have? Which has the greatest amount of memory? Do any come with software?

Computer Name	Price	Features

Fabricate

What will computers of the future look like? What special parts will be added? What will be the function of each? Design a new computer system for the year 2020. Label its special parts and explain what each does.

Cultural Connections

Feature

Appreciation of our multicultural heritage.

Find

Encyclopedia of World Cultures, by David Levinson.

Internet: Use any World Wide Web browser on the Internet to reach the American Special Collections of the Library of Congress. The address is: http://lcweb.loc.gov/spcoll/spclhome.html. Use the topics: Ethnic Groups, Cultures, History and Popular Culture.

Other Sources: Any encyclopedia if access to the World Wide Web on the Internet is not available.

Fanfare

In the early 1900s America was called the "great melting pot" as immigrants poured into this country from Europe. Thousands came to find new opportunities and a better way of life. They wanted to become Americans and blend in with the American way of life.

Our population is made up of people from all over the world. Instead of "melting" into this country they want to be Americans and still keep their individuality. Like a great "salad bowl," everything is mixed together, but you can still identify the individual ingredients.

We have a wonderful mixture of cultures. Our perspective becomes broadened as we learn about each other through the sharing of background and experiences. Using the December holidays, find out how different cultural groups celebrate. Create a flag design for each group with symbols that represent special observance features.

Fabricate

Pretend it is 1912 and you have just arrived in America from Europe. You are the only one of your family in this country. You do not speak English and have little money to spend. Write a letter home describing your feelings.

Customs, U.S.A.

Feature

Early American Customs.

Find

Colonial Living, by Edwin Tunis.

Everyday Life in Colonial America, by Louis B. Wright.

Other Sources: Any comprehensive history of colonial America.

Fanfare

Colonial shoes were made to fit either foot. By wearing them alternately left and then right, the shoes wore evenly and did not wear out as quickly.

To keep track of miles, "clacks" of each complete rotation of wagon wheels were counted. So many "clacks" equaled a mile. These were carved on stone or posts along Colonial roads providing information for travelers, thus the word "milestone."

What other unusual facts about early American life can you find? Collect them in a booklet and add illustrations. Share the booklet with others in your class or grade.

Fabricate

Find the phone number of a local historical society or museum. Set up a telephone interview to find out about early customs, events, or celebrations in your area. Are any architectural structures being restored? Are there any designated as landmarks? Compile a sightseeing brochure for visitors. You might call it a "Kid's View of (Your Town or City)."

Daily Doings

Feature

Use of an Almanac.

Find

Any current almanac, such as the *World Almanac*, or the *Universal Almanac*.

Fanfare

Almanac: "A calendar of the days, weeks, months of the year, that gives information about the weather, sunrise, sunset, important anniversaries, etc., during that period" (*Scholastic Dictionary of American English*).

Describe the events and information on your birthday. Include several from the day before and the day after.

Fabricate

Make some predictions for next year by using current almanacs.

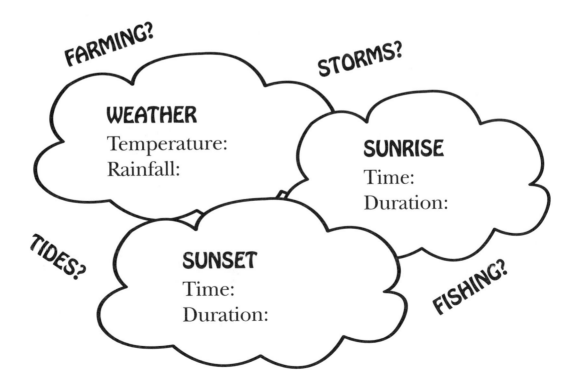

FARMING?

STORMS?

WEATHER
Temperature:
Rainfall:

SUNRISE
Time:
Duration:

TIDES?

SUNSET
Time:
Duration:

FISHING?

Environmental Embellishments

Feature

Environmental awareness.

Find

Dictionary of the Environment, edited by Michael Allaby

Readers' Guide to Periodical Literature

Other Sources: Free materials from local electric and gas utility companies.

Fanfare

As we share our space on earth with other living organisms, it is important to remember that all of us are using valuable resources. Available future resources will depend on how carefully we manage what we have today.

These are the "3 Rs" of conservation: REDUCE and use less resources by looking for alternative sources. REUSE articles by repairing rather than throwing away. RECYCLE things by finding new uses for them.

What is being done to save resources in your community? School? Home? Set up interviews with: the principal or someone in the administrative office, family members and friends, and call the utilities companies to find out what they are doing. Summarize all the information you gather by preparing a five minute talk for the class. Create graphs and other visual aids to accompany your speech.

Fabricate

Earth Day is celebrated each year on April 22. What special activities could the class get involved with to celebrate this special occasion? Describe each in an "earth circle" below.

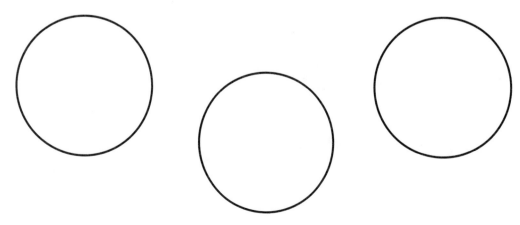

Family Findings

Feature

Genealogical research; writing letters for information.

Find

Guide to Genealogical Research in the National Archives.

The Researcher's Guide to American Genealogy, by Val Greenwood.

The Source: A Guidebook of American Genealogy, edited by Arlene Eakle and Johni Cerny

Where Did You Get Those Eyes? A Guide to Discovering Your Family History, by Kay Cooper.

Write to either of the following for free information:

National Archives
Reference Service Branch
Washington, DC 20408-0001

The National Genealogical Society
Educational Division
4527 Seventeenth St. North
Arlington, VA 22207-2399

Fanfare

Genealogy is the study of family histories. By researching letters, family bibles, birth and marriage certificates, land deeds, military records, and other family papers, one can determine a great deal about former family members. The largest collection of this type of information is contained in the Mormon Family History Library in Salt Lake City, Utah. Document information available dates from before 1900 on more than a million rolls of microfilm. Each year, over 30,000 new rolls are added. The library also houses over 200,000 volumes with records of over 10 million families and nearly 100 million names in the International Genealogic Index!

Create a "school tree" of records about yourself. List each grade you have been in, teachers you had, and subjects and your grades in each.

Fabricate

Librarians must also organize, catalogue, and collect many different kinds of materials. Interview the school librarian and find out how her job is similar to that of a genealogist. Plan your questions before the interview. Send a thank-you note afterwards!

Famous Firsts

Feature

First times; first events.

Find

Book of Answers, by Barbara Berliner.

Famous First Facts.

Facts on File Yearbook.

Other Sources: Any general encyclopedia.

Fanfare

The next time you enjoy an ice cream cone, you can thank a man selling sugar waffles at the St. Louis World's Fair in 1904. When one of the ice cream men ran out of serving dishes, the inventive waffle-maker got the idea to quickly roll his crisp fresh waffles into cone shapes. In this way they could sell ice cream to people–and it would not leak! The idea was an instant success.

Explain other firsts, such as who was the "home run king" of baseball, or what was the name of the first submarine built for use in war in 1776?

Fabricate

Be first! Invent and draw a new type of container for milk. Be sure to describe how it is opened and poured!

Future Fantasies

Feature

Future possibilities and predictions.

Find

Atlas of the Solar System, by Patrick Moore and Garry Hunt.
Student Handbook for the Study of the Future, by H. F. Didsbury.
Who's Who in Space.
Other Sources: *Readers' Guide to Periodical Literature* (any article on the future).

Fanfare

A Nobel Prize-winning author, John Galsworthy (1867–1963), was very interested in the future— its possibilities and benefits, as well as how people might accept changes they would have to make during the course of their lives. He once wrote: "If you do not think about the future, you cannot have one!"

Many futurists (people who think about the future by studying what we are doing today) see the future as a place where there will no longer be diseases, where people of all ages will be happy and learning, where our environment will be clean as we develop and use better energy sources. Make several future predictions based on the information you read in the areas of food, energy, and education.

Fabricate

Pretend you are part of a futuristic "Solution Seekers" company in the year 2050. Your job is to find solutions to problems people write you about. Brainstorm and suggest possible solutions for the following letter:

> Dear Solution Seekers, Inc.:
>
> We are all preparing for a long vacation to the Martian colony. Our children need interesting activities that will keep them entertained during the long trip. What should we do?
>
> Sincerely,
>
> Cosmo Dusto
>
> Mil Keeway
>
> Meetee Orite

Geologicals

Feature

Defining terms in an academic area.

Find

Any general dictionary such as *Webster's New World Dictionary*, or the *Random House Dictionary*.

Fanfare

Dictionaries are quick sources for defining words and providing information. Words such as *stalagmite, stalactite, limestone,* and *subterranean* have to do with speleology.

Define each term in italics above and try to guess what speleology is *before* looking it up. Combine the words into an adventure story article for a scientific magazine.

Fabricate

Read *Tom Sawyer* by Mark Twain. Illustrate the part of the story related to the terms you have just defined.

Holocaust

Feature

Understanding an event of World War II.

Find

American Jewish Yearbook, Vols. XXXI-XLVII.

Encyclopedia of the Holocaust, edited by Yisreal Gutman.

Write to:
The Simon Wiesenthal Center
9760 W. Pico Blvd.
Los Angeles, CA 90035

Other Sources: Any history of World War II that contains information on the Holocaust.

Fanfare

During World War II Adolf Hitler, the German Chancellor, believed that the "Aryan" race of Northern Europe should be purified. He wanted to segregate the population of each country his army conquered. Through the construction of concentration camps, Gypsies, political activists, the disabled and the Jews were singled out. In these camps over eleven million men, women and children were slaughtered. Six million were of the Jewish faith.

After the war, the allied nations conducted the Nuremberg Trials to bring to justice those accused of being involved in the "death camps." Holocaust studies remind us of this terrible period of history and of the importance of not forgetting what happened. Perhaps in this way we will never allow it to happen again and we will treat our fellow human beings with greater kindness and respect.

Find a copy of the *Diary of Anne Frank*. Read this true story of her experiences during the Holocaust. Share the book by preparing a book review for the class.

Fabricate

Create a "Bill of Human Rights." Include a list of behavior rules you think are important for all to follow. When the list is complete, share it with several classmates. Do they agree? Disagree? Why?

Incredible Edibles

Feature

Foods and their sources.

Find

Better Homes and Gardens New Junior Cook Book.

Columbia Encyclopedia of Nutrition.

Joy of Cooking.

New Food Book: Nutrition, Diet, Consumer Tips, and Food of the Future, by Melvin and Gilda Berger.

Other Sources: Any recent cookbook

Fanfare

People all over the world eat foods that seem strange to us, but are part of their normal diet. Examples are spicy curry in India, squid in Japan, congee (kon-je) rice cereal in China, and whale or seal fat in Alaska!

Select three of your favorite foods that might seem strange to a person from another country or culture. Brainstorm adjectives that might describe each.

Fabricate

Collect unusual recipes from cookbooks, magazines, and newspapers. Classify them according to the type of recipe, such as main dish, dessert, and so on. Design an "Incredible Edible" cookbook or recipe card file.

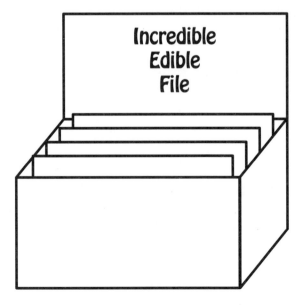

Language Lures

Feature

Fun with language forms and expressions.

Find

Brewer's Dictionary of Phrase and Fable.

Dictionary of American Regional English.

New Dictionary of American Slang.

Other Sources: Any special dictionary that addresses American idioms or analogies.

Fanfare

Our language is most confusing for others to learn. Besides the grammatical parts, there are many humorous and strange things we say. Visitors from other countries usually have a very difficult time communicating with Americans because of this. To make the problem worse, our everyday expressions constantly change. What was once "cool" or "neat" might be considered "rad" or "bad" or "def" at another time!

Make a list of expressions and their meanings from the 1940s or 1950s. Create an illustration for each. Start a "new" saying at your school by reviving an old one!

Fabricate

Set up categories in file folders. Place examples of each type of expression in the appropriate folder. Illustrations can be a humorous addition! Start a collection the class can add to during the year.

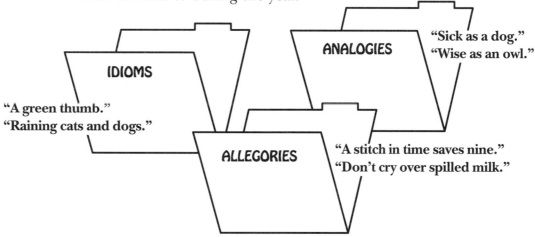

Magazine Mania

Feature

Awareness of the wide variety of available magazines.

Find

Assorted magazines of specialized and general interest.

Fanfare

Science, hobbies, sports, fashions, "how-to," the arts, puzzles, current events–the huge variety of available magazines is endless. Feature stories, pictures, and activities all provide us with knowledge and entertainment within the pages.

Survey your school library's magazines. Prepare a list of those you would suggest to other students your age. Briefly explain why you think each would be of interest.

Magazine	Reason

Fabricate

Take a "field trip" to a local newsstand. Which magazines are of interest to you? Which magazines deal only with sports? Hobbies? General interest? Report you findings to classmates.

Map Amusements

Feature

Atlas and map sources.

Find

Goode's World Atlas.

Hammond Citation World Atlas.

National Geographic Picture Atlas of Our World.

Webster's New Geographical Dictionary.

Other Sources: Assorted maps and atlases.

Fanfare

Maps are interesting to use, and provide us with a vast amount of information. No matter where a traveler might go, a map will be handy.

Have you ever noticed that many towns and cities in this country have very unusual names? How about Birdsnest, Virginia; Fruitland, Maryland; or Bird-In-Hand, Pennsylvania? Search through your research sources and compile a list of other unusually named places. Describe where each is and the nearest large city.

Fabricate

Create a catchy slogan for each of the unusual places that might attract visitors. Add other information tourists would want to know about and create an "Unusually Unusual Place" poster. Present it to a local travel agent when it is completed!

Musical Memories

Feature

Musicians and songs.

Find

American Popular Songs, edited by David Ewen.
Composers Since 1900.
Great Composers 1300-1900.
Popular American Composers.
Sing Together: Girl Scout Songbook

Fanfare

Music is the art of combining sound into different forms that are pleasing to the ear. From popular songs of each decade to great classical masterworks, music is part of man's creative spirit!

How are the lyrics of popular songs of the 1950s different from those of today? What is the title of the national anthem of a country you would like to visit? In a short paragraph, summarize the life of a composer who lived in the early 1800s.

Fabricate

Music is part of the everyday expressions we use. Think of some you can write in cut-out musical notes. Construct a musical mobile using the notes and other musical notations you find.

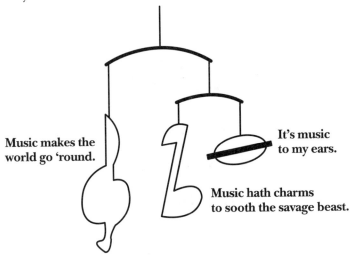

Music makes the world go 'round.

It's music to my ears.

Music hath charms to sooth the savage beast.

Nyms

Feature

Synonyms, acronyms, pseudonyms.

Find

Acronyms, Initialisms, and Abbreviations Dictionary.

Pseudonyms and Nicknames Dictionary.

Soules's Dictionary of English synonyms.

Other Sources: Any synonym and/or acronym dictionary.

Fanfare

"Nym" suffixes abound in our language: *Acronyms* are formed by using the first letter of each word in a phrase or group of related words. SCUBA is an acronym for *Self-Contained Underwater Breathing Apparatus*. NASA is the *National Aeronautics and Space Administration*.

Pseudonyms (literally, "false names") include the "pen names" often used by authors. "Mark Twain" was really Samuel Langhorne Clemens.

Among these and other "nyms," *synonyms* (different words that mean the same thing) are probably the most used. What can be done with *villainous, dreadful, foul, horrible, detestable?* Do they describe anything? Find out, combine them, use them in an "awfully" creative story!

Fabricate

Create a pseudonym for yourself as author of the "awful" story. Start your "awful" book with topics such as:

"An Awfully Funny Experience"

"An Awfully Scary Movie"

"An Awful Shirt I Own"

"The Awfully Hottest/Coldest Day of the Year"

Our Town

Feature

Using the phone book.

Find

Any telephone book.

Fanfare

A wealth of information exists in your phone book! Here you can find almost anything, from a friend's address to the nearest shoemaker or dentist. Need repairs? Clothing? Taxi service? Printing? Tutoring help? There is hardly a business of any kind that is not listed someplace within these wonderful pages!

Hunt through your phone book to fill in this chart.

Favorites	Name	Location	Phone Number
Friend			
Place to eat			
Place to shop			
School supplies			
Movie theatre			

Fabricate

Make a list of other types of information you found, such as maps and zip codes, street directories, coupons, etc.

People in Particular

Feature

Well-known people.

Find

American Nicknames.
Biography Index.
For the Record: Women in Sports.
Webster's Biographical Dictionary.

Fanfare

We can learn about some of the greatest people who ever lived by using the above-mentioned sources. The contributions of these people have made life better for all of us in spite of great difficulties some of them faced. They set high goals and followed their dreams!

- Albert Einstein did not speak until he was almost four years old! Where did he receive most of his training?

- "Babe" Zaharias received many awards in her lifetime. List several of these.

- What name was given to Benjamin Lynn? Why?

- Explain how you might find quick information about Charles A. Lindbergh.

Fabricate

If you had to set up a Hall of Fame of great Americans, who would you select? State five reasons or criteria you might use for their selection.

How could great people be described? Using the letters of G R E A T, think of several adjectives that start with each letter.

G _____

R _____

E _____

A _____

T _____

Places, Places, Places

Feature

States and countries of the world.

Find

Flags and American Arms Across the World.

State Names, Flags, Seals, Songs, Birds, Flowers and Other Symbols.

The Statesman's Year Book.

Other Sources: Any general encyclopedia yearbook.

Fanfare

We share planet Earth with billions of people. Have you ever wondered about what life might be like in another state? Another country? People of the world have many things in common with us–common needs and goals for themselves and their lives. Knowing something of other nations can bring about better understanding among people of the world.

Select a place at least 1,500 miles from where you live, and a place where you would like to visit or live in someday. Find out all you can about each and prepare a tape/filmstrip "travelogue" presentation to share with classmates.

Fabricate

Pretend you are an airline steward/stewardess talking to a group of tourists about to land in you selected state or country. Prepare a brief talk pointing out famous sights to see in each place and explaining how each place is similar to and different from your home area.

Presidents and Leaders

Feature

Presidents and well-known people.

Find

Facts About the Presidents.
Nobel Prize Winners.
U.S. Government Organization Manual.
Who's Who in America

Fanfare

"The executive power shall be vested in a President of the United States of America. He shall hold his office during the term of four years, and together with the Vice-President, chosen for the same term." (United States Constitution)

The Presidency of the United States of America is the highest office in the land, and the most weighty and responsible. Only those with a great sense of duty and willingness to serve have accepted this position. Great national and world events are usually part of every Presidential term. Go on a "fact hunt" and find events about several Presidents. Construct a time line showing the years of your selected Presidential terms.

Fabricate

"I do solemnly swear that I will faithfully execute the office of President of the United States, and will, to the best of my ability, preserve, protect, and defend the Constitution of the United States."

How does this oath of office compare to others you have taken in scouting or other clubs? Explain what you think is the most important part of taking any oath.

A Sampling of Sports

Feature

Everything about all kinds of sports.

Find

Encyclopedia of Sports.

Guinness Sports Record Book.

Sports, by Tim Hammond.

Sports and Games, by Harold Keith.

Other Sources: Any general sports encyclopedia.

Fanfare

Do you like to fish? Canoe? Play football or hockey? Just about every sport is covered in the above sources. For each sport you will find history and background, techniques for play, equipment, and scoring all thoroughly detailed.

Select a favorite sport and write a brief report covering the aspects of it that are new or different to you. Present the report in your physical education class. (Be sure to get permission from the coach or PE teacher first!)

Fabricate

Which sport do you consider the most unusual? The most dangerous? The most exciting? Prepare a display about "The Sport That Is the Most_____." Survey classmates for their opinions and show the completed data in graph form on a poster. Add it to your sports display.

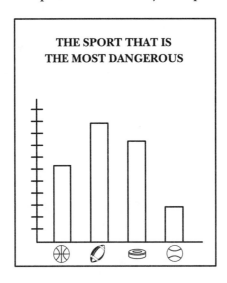

Sea Disasters

Feature

Sea disasters—an unusual source to find.

Find

Dictionary of Disasters at Sea During the Age of Steam (1824-1962), by Charles Hocking.

Rand McNally Atlas of the Oceans.

Reader's Digest Book of Facts.

Times Atlas of the Oceans.

Fanfare

On November 7, 1872, the *Mary Celeste* sailed from New York to Genoa with a cargo of crude alcohol. Aboard were Capt. B. S. Briggs, his wife and two-year-old daughter, and a crew of seven. On December 5th, about 590 miles west of Gibraltar, the ship was sighted and seemed to be in distress. Capt. Morehouse of the *Dei Gratia* ordered several men to investigate. Upon boarding the *Mary Celeste* they found no sign of damage to the ship, evidence of violence, or people present. The last log entry was November 24th. What happened still remains a mystery. Read more about their findings and present your own theory about what might have taken place during that strange voyage.

Fabricate

The *Titanic* and *Lusitania* are other examples of sea disasters. Read about each and explain the special laws enacted to prevent similar sea disasters in the future.

Research treasure ships sunk during the 1600s and 1700s and the efforts that recently brought about the salvage of many tons of their valuable cargo.

Special Events

Feature

Events for days of the year.

Find

The American Book of Days.
American Facts and Dates.
Famous First Facts.
Second Kids World Almanac of Records and Facts.

Fanfare

History is the sum total of man's deeds and his participation in events that have changed and shaped our world. By studying and analyzing the past, we gain better insights about our present and future.

What events occurred on your birthdate? On the first day of school? On Halloween? On Christmas Day? On the birthday of a relative or friend? Construct a birthdate calendar for people you know.

Fabricate

Design a birthday button. Use symbols representing life events. What might represent you favorite toy? First word? First step? Favorite trip? Birthday?

Unusual and Strange

Feature

World records.

Find

Guinness Book of World Records.
Macmillan Book of Fascinating Facts.
Second Kids World Almanac of Records and Facts.

Fanfare

Benjamin Guinness collected and wrote his first book to help settle arguments people were having about record-setting events and those who set them. The first book, published in 1955, was 198 pages long. It was so popular that it has since been published in 10 different countries and has grown to over 700 pages. It is the top-selling copyrighted book in the history of publications! By 1986, so many had been sold through the years that they would equal 118 stacks each as high as Mt. Everest (29,028 feet)!

Describe any three unusual record-setting events found in the Guinness book. Explain what the event was, who the participant(s) were and what category it was part of. Combine your information and write a "newspaper" article about it. Add an illustration of what took place.

Fabricate

What new world record would you like to set? How would you go about doing this and proving it took place? (Consult the first few pages of the book to find out.) Set up a plan of action to set your own record!

My Plan:

Step 1	Step 3
Step 2	Step 4

What Did You Say?

Feature

Foreign language meanings, phrases, and abbreviations.

Find

Dictionary of Foreign Phrases and Abbreviations, by Kevin Guinagh.

New Dictionary of American Slang.

Soule's Dictionary of English Synonyms.

Other Sources: Any recent dictionary of foreign phrases.

Fanfare

The number of Americans traveling beyond the borders of the United States grows each year. Foreign travel is a popular vacation goal. One of the main difficulties for travelers is the ability to communicate with someone who speaks a language other than English. Handy sources of various languages are available and new minicomputers translate words and phrases in several languages.

Make a list of all the questions you think would be important to ask someone if you were visiting a foreign country. For example, you might want to know about a restaurant, hotel, or transportation!

Fabricate

Sometimes the pronunciation of a word or phrase will have similarities from country to country. Look at the foreign words below. The English word is "school."

Language	Written	Pronounced
French	ecole	eh-kohl
Spanish	escuela	ehs-kweh-lah
Italian	scuola	skoo-oh-lah
Hawaiian	kula	koo-lah

Add to the list by finding "school" in other languages. Select another commonly used noun and compare it the same way.

Do you think all languages have such similarities? What might be the reason? Research *word origins* for some of the possibilities.

Who Said That?

Feature

Memorable quotations.

Find

Bartlett's Familiar Quotations, by John Bartlett.

Home Book of Quotations, edited by Burton Stevenson.

Oxford Dictionary of Quotations.

Other Sources: Any recent quotation dictionary

Fanfare

Webster's Dictionary of the English Language, Revised Edition, May 1979, states the following: "Quote: to repeat the words of another person or passage from a book, poem, etc. Quotations: a quoting of someone else's words. Quotable: such as may be repeated, suitable or worthy of quoting."

One quote listed under the great English author Charles Dickens is: "A smattering of everything and a knowledge of nothing." Read the quotes related to knowledge and learning at the beginning of this book. How do they compare with Dickens' quote? Compose an essay summarizing their meaning.

Fabricate

Search through *Bartlett's* for appropriate quotes that might be used in the school library, principal's office, guidance office, cafeteria, classroom, and your own room at home. Write them out on large banners suitable for hanging and add symbols or illustrative designs. Bring them around as your personal gift to each place!

Write Away

Feature

Sources for free information.

Find

Stationery!

Fanfare

Free materials are plentiful! All you need to do is write a letter (use the business form), address an envelope, and add a stamp. Within weeks you will receive some great information in the mail that you can use for research. The Internet is another place where free information can be located or requested. Try using your browser on the World Wide Web, and search for an interesting subject, or check a guide to the Internet to find a specific address on the Web.

Fabricate

At the time of this writing, all addresses are active. Please remember that agencies do move or are changed from time to time. Another good source of names and addresses is the *Educators' Index of Free Material*, edited by May P. Parent (Randolph, WI: Educators' Progress League.)

Look for specific topics you are interested in. As time passes, your file of addresses and materials can be expanded for future sources.

Animals/Pets

Animal Protection Inst. of America
2831 Fruit Ridge Road
Sacramento, CA 95820

The Bronx Zoo
N.Y. Zoological Society
185th St. & Southern Blvd.
Bronx, NY 10460

Arts

Metropolitan Museum of Art
Educational Department
1000 Fifth Ave.
New York, NY 10028

National Portrait Gallery
Public Affairs Office
Eighth & F Sts., NW
Washington, DC 20560

Authors

Writers Guild of America
Educational Department
555 West 57th St.
New York, NY 10019

Children's Book Council
568 Broadway
New York, NY 10012

Birds

National Audubon Society
950 Third Ave.
New York, NY 10022

Circus

Ringling Bros. & Barnum & Bailey Circus
Dept. of Educational Services
86 Westwood Ctr. Dr.
Vienna, VA 22182

Clown College
140 Ringling Drive South
Venice, FL 33595

Communications

CBS-TV
7800 Beverly Blvd.
Los Angeles, CA 90036

NBC-TV
3000 W. Alameda Ave.
Burbank, CA 91523

Conservation

Sierra Club
730 Polk St.
San Francisco, CA 94109

Nat'l. Parks & Conservation Assn.
1776 Massachusetts Ave., NW
Suite 200
Washington, DC 20036

Cultural Studies/Social Science

United Nations Association of the U.S.A.
Free Literature Department
485 5th Ave., 2nd Fl.
New York, NY 10017

UNESCO Assn. of the U.S.A.
5815 Lawton Ave.
Oakland, CA 94618-1510

Flight/Aviation

United Airlines
1200 E. Algonquin Rd.
Elk Grove Village, IL 60007

Civil Air Patrol
Bldg. 714
Maxwell AFB, AL 36112-5572

Health/Nutrition

Kellogg Company
Educational Division
1 Kellog Ave.
Battle Creek, MI 49016

National Dairy Council
10255 W. Higgins Rd.
Rosemont, IL 60018-5616

Insects

Publications Department
Office of Communications
U.S. Department of Agriculture
14th & Independence Ave., SW
Washington, DC 20250

Inventions

U.S. Department of Commerce
Office of Public Affairs
Patent and Trademark Office
Washington, DC 20231

Invent America!
510 King St., Suite 420
Alexandria, VA 22314

Law

Department of the Treasury
U.S. Secret Service
1800 G St., NW, Rm 800
Washington, DC 20233

The FBI
U.S. Department of Justice
10th & Pennsylvania Ave., NW
Washington, DC 20535

American Bar Association
Division of Communication
750 N. Lake Shore Dr.
Chicago, IL 60611

Patriotism

Veterans of Foreign Wars of the U.S.A.
200 Maryland Ave., NE
Washington, DC 20002

Sea

U.S. Department of Transportation
Maritime Division
400 7th St., SW, Ste. 7206
Washington, DC 20590

Greenpeace, USA
1436 U St., NW
Washington, DC 20009

Space

NASA
Educational Material Dept.
Lyndon B. Johnson Space Center
Huston, TX 77058

Smithsonian Astrophyics
Obervatory
Publications Dept.
60 Garden St.
Cambridge, MA 02138

Sports

U.S. Olympic Committee
Olympic Plaza
Colorado Springs, CO 80909-5760

National League of
Professional Baseball Clubs
350 Park Ave., 18th Fl.
New York, NY 10022

Weather

Environmental Data Service
Boulder, CO 80302

Student Reference Activities

Tracking Chart

Name _____   Grade _____

ACTIVITY TITLE	DATE STARTED	FANFARE	FABRICATE	DATE COMPLETED

Teacher Signature _____

Answers for "People in Particular"

Einstein received most of his training in Vienna, Austria, and Germany.

"Babe" Zaharias, or Mildred Ella Didriksen Zaharias, was an All-American Basketball player in 1930; won eight events in women's national track and field for two years; captured two events in the 1932 Olympics, setting new world records; became the leading women's golfer in the U.S., winning 17 titles in a row; and in 1954 won the U.S. National Open and the All-American Open.

Benjamin Lynn was given the name of the Daniel Boone of Kentucky. He was really a preacher.

Quick information about Lindbergh can be found in *Webster's Biographical Dictionary.*

Recommended Reference Resources

Please note that these are suggested titles, and that all are not required for the student activities. See the FIND section of each featured topic for alternative titles. In addition, most of the following titles are frequently revised, and new editions may have new editors or revised titles. For those reasons, specific editions and copyright dates are not cited. The activities in *Pardon Me, But Your References Are Showing* are general in nature, and any relatively recent edition can be used.

Title Index

Author/Subject Index